The Key Principles From Oliver Burkeman Meditations For Mortals

Four Weeks to Embrace Your Limitations and Make Time for What Counts

Justty Rachy

TABLE OF CONTENTS

2 The Key Principles

INTRODUCTION

Welcome to the Journey

In a world that constantly urges us to chase after more
time, more success, and more control, we often lose
sight of an essential truth: life is finite. The Key
Principles from Meditations for Mortals invites you to
step back from the relentless race and embrace the
reality of your limitations. This book is not about doing
more or stretching yourself thinner; instead, it offers a
radical shift in perspective. It challenges you to embrace
your mortality, to recognize that your time on Earth is
limited, and to live fully within that constraint. In doing
so, you'll discover that limitations are not barriers, but
tools for leading a more intentional and meaningful life.

Why Limitations Are Your Greatest Asset

Many view limitations as weaknesses—whether it's the
finite number of hours in a day, the unpredictability of
life, or our eventual end. Yet, these very limit youations
are what give life its urgency, depth, and significance.
Imagine if time were unlimited. Would we still feel driven
to make meaningful decisions? Would we pursue our

deepest passions with the same fervor? In this book, you'll learn how acknowledging your limits leads to clarity, creativity, and fulfillment. By understanding that we cannot do everything, we become empowered to focus on what truly matters.

Embracing Time as Finite

Our society often encourages us to think of time as something we can manipulate, extend, or outsmart. But what if the key to living well lies in accepting time for what it is—a finite resource? This book offers a fresh perspective on time management, not as a way to squeeze more into your day, but as a framework for prioritizing what counts. You'll explore how making peace with time's limits can help you let go of unnecessary stress and expectations. Instead of fighting against time, you'll learn to use it with intention, ensuring that your limited hours, days, and years are spent on what brings meaning and joy.

How This Book Will Transform Your Relationship with Life

Over the course of four weeks, The Key Principles Meditations for Mortals will guide you through practical exercises and philosophical insights designed to shift your mindset. You'll begin by facing the reality of your mortality and learning to view it not with fear, but with a sense of liberation. From there, you'll explore how to sharpen your focus, make more deliberate choices, and live within constraints that foster freedom, creativity, and fulfillment. This journey is about much more than just time management. It's about living with purpose and clarity, understanding that your life is defined by what you choose to do with the time you have.

By the end of this book, you will have developed a deeper understanding of what it means to live well in the face of life's ultimate limitation: time itself. You'll emerge not just with strategies to manage your days more effectively, but with a renewed sense of meaning and direction.

5 The Key Principles

WEEK 1

THE POWER OF LIMITS

Accepting the Boundaries of Existence

Facing the Reality of Mortality
The first step in this journey is to confront one of life's most uncomfortable truths: your own mortality. As humans, we tend to avoid thinking about death, often seeing it as a distant event. However, coming to terms with the fact that life is finite can radically change how we live. In this chapter, you'll be guided through reflections that bring death into the conversation, not to evoke fear, but to invite awareness. This is not about morbid preoccupation, but about a perspective shift that helps you recognize that every day is precious. By accepting your mortality, you'll discover a new sense of clarity about what really matters.

Reframing Scarcity: Why Less Time Is More

Time is often viewed as something we lack—there's never enough of it, and we constantly wish for more. However, scarcity can be a blessing in disguise. When we realize that time is limited, we are forced to make decisions with intention. This chapter will help you reframe the concept of scarcity, showing that limitations push us to choose what's essential, and in doing so, enrich our lives. You'll explore how the very fact that you don't have endless time can lead to deeper satisfaction by prompting you to focus on the most important aspects of your life, relationships, and goals.

Learning to Say No: A Skill for Embracing Priorities
One of the most practical tools in managing your limitations is learning how to say "no." Often, we feel obligated to say "yes" to everything—every project, every opportunity, every request. But in reality, each "yes" spreads your focus thinner and pulls you away from your core priorities. In this chapter, you'll learn why saying "no" is one of the most empowering actions you can take. By embracing this simple word, you'll protect your time and energy for the things that truly matter to you. You'll explore strategies for how to gracefully say

7 The Key Principles

"no" in both personal and professional settings, without guilt or resentment.

The Paradox of Control: How Letting Go Empowers You
We often seek control over our lives, believing that the more we can manage, the better things will turn out. But what if true empowerment comes from letting go of the need to control everything? This chapter delves into the paradox of control, revealing how releasing your grip on the uncontrollable aspects of life can lead to freedom and peace of mind. You'll learn how to differentiate between what is within your control and what is not, and how to focus your energy on the former while accepting the latter. By doing so, you'll find that life flows more easily, and you'll be better equipped to handle its inevitable uncertainties.

Reflection Practice: Journaling on Daily Limits
The week concludes with a reflection exercise designed to deepen your understanding of the themes you've explored. You'll be invited to journal about the limits you encounter daily, whether they are time constraints, physical boundaries, or emotional challenges. Through this practice, you'll begin to notice how embracing these

limits rather than resisting them leads to greater clarity and peace. By regularly reflecting on your limitations, you'll cultivate an ongoing awareness of how to live more purposefully within the boundaries life sets for you.

Week 1 sets the foundation for embracing the power of limits by helping you shift your mindset from seeing constraints as obstacles to recognizing them as guiding principles. By the end of this week, you will have developed a deeper acceptance of mortality, a sharper focus on what truly matters, and a clearer understanding of how to use your limits to your advantage.

1. How would your daily decisions and priorities change if you fully embraced the reality of your mortality, knowing that each moment is both precious and fleeting?

_____

_____

_____

_____

_____

2. In what areas of your life have you been viewing time as a scarcity, and how could reframing that scarcity as a positive force help you focus more on what truly matters?

_____

_____

_____

_____

3. Reflect on the times you've said "yes" out of obligation or guilt. How might your life improve if you mastered the art of saying "no" to protect your time and

energy?

_____

_____

_____

_____

_____

4. How has the pursuit of control over every aspect of your life created unnecessary stress or frustration? What could you gain by letting go and accepting the limits of what you can control?

_____

_____

_____

_____

5. As you reflect on your daily limits, how do these boundaries—whether in time, energy, or capability—guide you toward greater clarity and purpose, rather than restricting your potential?

WEEK 2

MASTERING THE ART OF FOCUS

Shifting from Productivity to Purpose

The Myth of Multitasking: How Distraction Steals Your Life

In a world that constantly encourages multitasking, we've come to believe that doing more at once is a sign of efficiency. However, research shows that multitasking is a myth—it actually reduces productivity and fragments your attention, leaving you mentally drained and less focused on what matters. This chapter delves into the neuroscience behind focus, explaining how multitasking sabotages your ability to perform at your best. You'll learn to recognize the hidden cost of distractions and understand why doing one thing at a time—single-tasking—leads to deeper engagement, more creativity, and greater satisfaction.

13 The Key Principles

Choosing What Counts: Narrowing Down the Essentials
If time is limited, then how you spend it becomes crucial. But with so many demands on your attention, how do you decide what deserves your focus? This chapter offers practical strategies for identifying your core priorities—the people, projects, and passions that truly matter. You'll explore frameworks for assessing what's essential versus what's merely urgent, and you'll learn how to create a life that reflects your deepest values, not just the demands of the moment. By narrowing down your focus, you'll reclaim time for the things that bring you the most meaning and joy.

Time Boxing Your Day: Structuring for Meaning, Not Just Efficiency
Once you've identified your priorities, the challenge becomes protecting them amidst the chaos of daily life. Enter time boxing—a simple but powerful method for scheduling your day around your core activities. Time boxing involves setting aside specific blocks of time for focused work, personal projects, or meaningful leisure, ensuring that you make deliberate use of your hours. This chapter provides a step-by-step guide to

implementing time boxing, helping you move from reactive busyness to proactive purpose. Rather than using your time for efficiency's sake, you'll learn to structure it for maximum meaning.

The Gift of Slowness: Cultivating Mindful Presence
In a culture obsessed with speed and productivity, slowing down can feel counterintuitive, even lazy. But the truth is, moving slower often leads to better outcomes. This chapter explores the concept of "mindful presence"—the ability to be fully engaged in the present moment, whether you're working, spending time with loved ones, or simply enjoying solitude. You'll discover how slowing down enhances your focus, reduces stress, and allows for more thoughtful decision-making. By cultivating slowness, you'll tap into a deeper sense of calm and fulfillment, becoming more present in the activities that matter most to you.

Reflection Practice: Mind Mapping Your Priorities
At the end of this week, you'll engage in a reflection exercise designed to solidify the lessons learned. Mind mapping is a creative, visual way to organize your thoughts and goals. You'll be guided through the

15 The Key Principles

process of creating a mind map that highlights your top priorities, showing how they connect to your broader life purpose. This exercise will help you visually break down complex ideas into manageable actions, reinforcing your focus on the essentials. Through this practice, you'll develop a clearer roadmap for how to structure your time and energy moving forward.

Week 2 is all about refining your focus and ensuring that your time and attention are spent on what truly counts. By eliminating distractions, narrowing down priorities, and embracing a more deliberate pace of life, you'll move from a reactive state of busyness to a proactive, purposeful way of living.

1. How do you typically respond to cravings or difficult emotions? Can you think of a time when being mindful or compassionate to yourself could have changed the outcome?

_____

_____

2. In what areas of your recovery journey have you been
the hardest on yourself? How might embracing
self-compassion create space for healing and growth?

_____

_____

_____

_____

_____

3. When you practise mindfulness, what distractions or
uncomfortable thoughts arise? How can observing these
without judgement help you in overcoming addiction?

_____

_____

17 The Key Principles

_____

_____

_____

4. How do you view your relationship with setbacks in your recovery? What would it look like if you responded to these setbacks with kindness rather than criticism?

_____

_____

_____

_____

5. What daily habits or routines can you incorporate to remind yourself to stay present and mindful? How could small moments of mindfulness transform your overall

progress?

_____

_____

_____

_____

_____

WEEK 3

FINDING FREEDOM IN CONSTRAINTS

How Structure Leads to Creativity and Fulfilment

The Value of Boundaries: Why Freedom Needs Form
We often think of freedom as the ability to do whatever we want, whenever we want. But too much freedom can actually be overwhelming. Without boundaries, it's hard to know where to focus, and we can end up wasting time on things that don't matter. This chapter explains how setting boundaries—whether it's limiting your work hours, defining your personal space, or sticking to routines—actually creates more freedom. With clear limits in place, you'll have more mental energy and time for the things that really matter to you. Boundaries, instead of restricting you, give you structure and direction, which leads to more fulfilling choices.

Creating Your Personal Philosophy of Time

Everyone has their own relationship with time. Some people are always in a rush, while others are more laid-back. But if you don't consciously think about how you view and use time, you can end up feeling like you're constantly behind or wasting your life. In this chapter, you'll be encouraged to reflect on your personal beliefs about time and create a "philosophy" that guides how you use it. Do you want to be someone who prioritizes family, work, relaxation, or learning? By getting clear on what matters most to you, you can start shaping your daily routine in a way that aligns with your values.

Rituals and Routines: Building Anchors in the Chaos

Life can be unpredictable, with constant distractions and unexpected challenges. That's where routines come in. Having daily or weekly rituals—like a morning walk, dedicated work hours, or family dinners—gives you stability and keeps you grounded even when things get busy. This chapter explores how creating simple, consistent routines can reduce stress and help you stay focused on what matters. These rituals serve as "anchors" in your day, making it easier to manage your time and energy without feeling overwhelmed. You'll learn practical tips for building routines that fit your lifestyle and help you make progress on your goals.

The Unexpected Joy of Limitation: Less Is Truly More
It's easy to think that having more time, money, or options would automatically make life better. But sometimes, having too much can lead to decision fatigue, distractions, and stress. This chapter flips the script, showing that having less—less on your schedule, fewer distractions, or even fewer possessions—can actually make you happier. You'll explore the concept of "voluntary simplicity," which means choosing to limit certain things in your life so you can focus on what's truly important. By embracing limitations, you'll experience more freedom, clarity, and joy in your daily life.

Reflection Practice: Designing Your Ideal Week
At the end of this week, you'll take time to design your "ideal week." This exercise is about imagining what your perfect week would look like if you could focus only on what's most important to you. What would your

mornings look like? How much time would you spend on work, hobbies, or relationships? By mapping out this ideal week, you'll have a blueprint for how to create more balance, fulfilment, and freedom in your actual life. It's not about perfection, but about creating a realistic guide to help you live in line with your priorities.

Week 3 helps you see that limits aren't something to fear—they're tools that can guide you toward a more focused, fulfilling life. By setting boundaries, building routines, and embracing simplicity, you can create the freedom to live the life you truly want.

1. How have the absence of clear boundaries in your life contributed to stress or confusion, and what specific limits could you set to gain more freedom and focus?

_____

_____

_____

_____

2. What is your personal philosophy about time? How would your daily routine change if you started living in a way that truly reflects your core values and priorities?

_____

_____

_____

_____

_____

3. Think about a routine or ritual you've followed in the past. How did it help you stay grounded amidst the chaos, and how could introducing more rituals improve your current life balance?

_____

_____

_____

_____

_____

4. In what areas of your life could embracing limitations—like fewer distractions or simpler routines—actually lead to more freedom and joy, rather than feeling restricted?

_____

_____

_____

_____

_____

5. As you design your "ideal week," what priorities emerge that you've been neglecting, and how can you start integrating them into your life to create a better balance and fulfilment?

_____

25 The Key Principles

26 The Key Principles

WEEK 4

EMBRACING THE IMPERMANENCE OF LIFE

Living Fully in a World of Constant Change

Accepting Change as a Constant
One of the hardest lessons in life is realizing that nothing stays the same. Everything we experience—our relationships, careers, even our emotions—is in a constant state of change. This chapter helps you come to terms with the fact that impermanence is a fundamental part of life. By embracing this truth instead of resisting it, you'll learn to live more fully in the present moment, letting go of the fear of losing what you have. The more you accept that change is inevitable, the easier it becomes to navigate life's transitions with grace.

Letting Go of Perfectionism

We often hold onto the idea that if we can just get everything perfect—our work, our relationships, ourselves—then we'll be truly happy. But perfection is an illusion, and chasing it only leads to stress and dissatisfaction. This chapter invites you to let go of the need for everything to be flawless and to embrace the beauty of imperfection. You'll discover that life is richer and more rewarding when you stop trying to control every detail and allow things to unfold naturally, even when they're messy or uncertain.

Facing Loss and Grief

Change isn't always easy, especially when it involves loss. Whether it's the end of a relationship, the loss of a job, or the death of a loved one, grief is a natural part of life's transitions. This chapter provides insights on how to face loss with courage and compassion. You'll learn that grief is not something to "get over" but rather something to experience fully. By allowing yourself to feel your emotions instead of pushing them away, you'll move through grief in a healthier, more healing way.

Learning to Live Lightly

When we hold on too tightly to things—whether material possessions, ideas, or expectations—we make it harder for ourselves to adapt to life's changes. This chapter encourages you to adopt a mindset of "living lightly." This doesn't mean caring less, but rather, being less attached to outcomes and more open to whatever life brings. By living lightly, you'll free yourself from the weight of constant worry and control, making it easier to go with the flow and find peace in the present moment.

Reflection Practice: Writing a Letter to Your Future Self To wrap up the final week, you'll engage in a powerful reflection exercise by writing a letter to your future self. This letter will serve as a reminder of the lessons you've learned throughout the four weeks, as well as your hopes and intentions for the future. What advice would you give your future self about handling change? What do you hope you'll have learned or experienced by then? By putting these thoughts into writing, you'll create a lasting connection to the person you are now and the person you're becoming.

Week 4 is about learning to flow with life's changes instead of fighting against them. By accepting impermanence, letting go of perfectionism, facing grief with compassion, and living lightly, you'll find a deeper sense of peace and fulfillment, no matter what life throws your way.

1. How do you perceive your limitations in life, and in what ways can embracing these limitations lead to a more fulfilling existence?

_____

_____

_____

_____

_____

2. Reflect on a recent experience where you felt overwhelmed by choices. How did this impact your ability to focus on what truly matters, and what strategies can you implement to simplify your decision-making process?

_____

_____

_____

_____

_____

3. What practices can you incorporate into your daily routine to cultivate a deeper sense of gratitude for the present moment, and how might this shift your perspective on life?

_____

_____

_____

_____

_____

4. Consider a fear or uncertainty you are currently facing. How might reframing your relationship with this fear lead to personal growth or unexpected opportunities?

_____

_____

_____

_____

_____

5. In what ways can you intentionally strengthen your connections with others this week, and how might these relationships contribute to a more meaningful and fulfilling life?

_____

_____

_____

33 The Key Principles

CONCLUSION

"The Key Principles from Meditations for Mortals: Four Weeks to Embrace Your Limitations and Make Time for What Counts" serves as a powerful reminder that our time is finite, and how we choose to spend it shapes the essence of our lives. Acknowledging our limitations is not a weakness but a profound strength that enables us to focus on what truly matters.

Through self-reflection and intentional living, we learn to prioritise our values, nurture meaningful relationships, and embrace the present moment. Each week guides us toward a deeper understanding of ourselves, encouraging us to confront our fears, simplify our choices, and cultivate gratitude.

As we internalise these principles, we realize that fulfilment does not stem from relentless striving or the accumulation of achievements, but rather from our ability to connect, love, and appreciate the beauty in everyday life. This journey invites us to let go of perfectionism, embrace vulnerability, and find joy in our shared humanity.

Ultimately, these teachings inspire us to live authentically and purposefully, transforming our limitations into opportunities for growth and connection. By making time for what truly counts, we not only enrich our own lives but also contribute to a more compassionate and meaningful world.

Made in United States
Orlando, FL
13 December 2024